SCIENCE ESSENTIALS

EARTH AND ATMOSPHERE

This book belongs to

Wonder House

EARTH AND ATMOSPHERE

EARTH, OUR HOME,
IS SPECIAL AND JUST ONE

THE THIRD PLANET FROM
THE SUN

WITH AIR, WATER, SOIL,
SUNLIGHT AND TREES

IT'S A PERFECT PLACE FOR
YOU AND ME

LET'S MAKE IT EVEN
MORE WONDERFUL AND
NOT LITTER AWAY

AND REMEMBER THAT
EVERY DAY IS AN EARTH DAY!

EARTH DAY
We are all crew members on spaceship earth.
5 WAYS TO MAKE EARTH A BETTER PLACE.
CONTEST
JENNY, WHAT IS EARTH DAY ALL ABOUT?
RON, IT MARKS THE START OF AN ENVIRONMENTAL MOVEMENT IN 1970. IT IS CELEBRATED TO PROMOTE CONCERN FOR OUR UNIQUE PLANET, EARTH.

UNIQUE PLANET? WHAT MAKES THE EARTH UNIQUE?
LET ME TELL YOU WHY EARTH IS UNIQUE.

WHAT IS EARTH?

EARTH IS THE PLANET WE LIVE ON, ONE OF THE EIGHT PLANETS IN OUR SOLAR SYSTEM AND THE ONLY KNOWN PLACE IN THE UNIVERSE TO SUPPORT LIFE. EARTH IS THE THIRD PLANET FROM THE SUN.

QUICK FACTS ABOUT THE EARTH

NAME

DERIVED FROM THE ENGLISH-GERMAN WORD 'ERDE' WHICH MEANS GROUND/SOIL.

SHAPE

NOT A PERFECT SPHERE. IT IS LIKE AN ORANGE-FLAT AT THE POLES AND BULGES AT THE EQUATOR.

SIZE

FIFTH LARGEST PLANET WITH EQUATORIAL RADIUS-6,378 KM

COSMIC COMPANION

EARTH HAS ONE NATURAL SATELLITE-THE MOON

EARTH'S DISTANCE FROM THE SUN

93 MILLION MILES
(150 MILLION KM)

NORTH POLE

THE NORTHERNMOST PART OF THE EARTH.

EQUATOR

THE EQUATOR IS AN IMAGINARY LINE THAT RUNS THROUGH THE MIDDLE OF THE EARTH. IT DIVIDES THE EARTH INTO TWO EQUAL HALVES.

AXIS

IT IS AN IMAGINARY LINE AROUND WHICH THE EARTH SPINS. EARTH'S AXIS IS TILTED AT ABOUT 23.5 DEGREES.

SOUTH POLE

THE SOUTHERNMOST PART OF THE EARTH.

ORBIT

IT IS THE PATH THAT THE EARTH TAKES AS IT MOVES AROUND THE SUN. EARTH'S ORBIT IS ELLIPTICAL.

DAYS AND YEARS

A DAY ON EARTH IS 24 HOURS. EARTH MAKES A COMPLETE ORBIT AROUND THE SUN IN 365 DAYS, WHICH IS A YEAR ON EARTH.

EARTH IS THE ONLY PLANET IN THE SOLAR SYSTEM WHOSE NAME DIDN'T ORIGINATE FROM GRECO-ROMAN MYTHOLOGY.

SURFACE

EARTH IS A ROCKY PLANET WITH A SOLID SURFACE.

SURFACE OF THE EARTH

EARTH HAS A SOLID SURFACE WITH DIFFERENT LANDFORMS AND WATER BODIES.

ABOUT 71% OF THE EARTH'S SURFACE IS COVERED WITH WATER IN THE FORM OF DIFFERENT WATER BODIES.

ONLY 29% OF THE EARTH'S SURFACE IS COVERED WITH LAND. THE LAND IS SPLIT INTO LARGE MASSES CALLED CONTINENTS.

LAYERS OF THE EARTH

EARTH IS MADE UP OF A NUMBER OF ROCKY LAYERS. THESE LAYERS CAN BE DIVIDED INTO THREE MAIN PARTS—CRUST, MANTLE AND CORE.

CRUST

IT IS THE OUTERMOST LAYER OF THE EARTH.

THICKNESS: VARIES FROM 30-70 KM BELOW THE LAND AND 6-12 KM BELOW THE OCEANS.

MADE UP OF: DIFFERENT KINDS OF ROCKS.

MANTLE

IT IS THE SECOND LAYER OF THE EARTH.

HAS TWO PARTS: UPPER MANTLE AND LOWER MANTLE

THICKNESS: 2,900 KM

MADE UP OF: VERY HOT, MOSTLY SOLID ROCK.

CORE

IT IS THE INNERMOST LAYER OF THE EARTH.

HAS TWO PARTS: OUTER CORE AND INNER CORE

THICKNESS: OUTER CORE—2,300 KM, INNER CORE—1,220 KM

MADE UP OF: MELTED IRON AND NICKEL (OUTER CORE)

SOLID METAL: MOSTLY IRON (INNER CORE)

THE CRUST AND THE UPPER MANTLE TOGETHER FORM THE LITHOSPHERE.

WHAT ALL CAN WE FIND ON THE EARTH?

EARTH CONSISTS OF LAND, WATER, AIR AND LIFE.

THE LAND ON EARTH IS NOT THE SAME EVERYWHERE; IT EXISTS IN DIFFERENT FORMS. THESE ARE CALLED LANDFORMS.

LANDFORMS ON EARTH INCLUDES

SOURCES OF WATER ON EARTH INCLUDE

AIR ON EARTH IS MADE UP OF DIFFERENT GASES.

LIFE ON EARTH INCLUDES HUMANS, PLANTS AND ANIMALS. THERE ARE MILLIONS OF SPECIES OF LIVING BEINGS ON EARTH. THEY RANGE FROM TINY CREATURES TO VERY LARGE ONES.

CONTINENTS AND OCEANS

CONTINENTS ARE HUGE MASSES OF LAND THAT ARE SEPARATED FROM EACH OTHER BY WATER OR ANY OTHER NATURAL FEATURE. THERE ARE SEVEN CONTINENTS ON THE EARTH.

ASIA IS THE LARGEST CONTINENT AND AUSTRALIA IS THE SMALLEST.

ANTARCTICA AND AUSTRALIA ARE SEPARATED FROM THE OTHER CONTINENTS BY OCEANS. THE OTHER FIVE CONTINENTS ARE JOINED TO AT LEAST ONE OTHER CONTINENT BY LAND.

OCEANS ARE LARGE WATER BODIES OF SALT WATER ON THE EARTH. THERE ARE FIVE OCEANS—ATLANTIC, PACIFIC, INDIAN, ARCTIC AND SOUTHERN.

SEA IS A PART OF AN OCEAN THAT IS PARTLY SURROUNDED BY LAND.

SOME OF THE NAVIGATED SEAS ARE RED SEA, BLACK SEA, MEDITERRANEAN SEA, CASPIAN SEA, BAY OF BENGAL, ARABIAN SEA, SARGASSO SEA AND CARIBBEAN SEA.

THE PACIFIC OCEAN IS THE LARGEST OF ALL OCEANS.

THE ARCTIC OCEAN IS FROZEN AND COVERED WITH ICE THROUGHOUT THE YEAR.

MOVEMENTS OF THE EARTH!

LIKE OTHER PLANETS, THE EARTH MOVES IN TWO WAYS—ONE ON ITS AXIS AND ANOTHER AROUND THE SUN.

ROTATION

THE EARTH SPINS ON ITS AXIS. THIS MOVEMENT IS CALLED ROTATION.

EARTH MAKES A FULL SPIN AROUND ITS AXIS ONCE EVERY 24 HOURS. THESE 24 HOURS MAKE A DAY ON EARTH.

WHY DO WE HAVE DAY AND NIGHT?

AS THE EARTH SPINS, ONE OF ITS SIDES FACES THE SUN, WHILE THE OTHER FACES AWAY.

THE SIDE OF THE EARTH FACING THE SUN RECEIVES HEAT AND LIGHT OF THE SUN. WE EXPERIENCE DAY HERE.

THE SIDE OF THE EARTH FACING AWAY INTO SPACE DOESN'T RECEIVE SUNLIGHT AND IS DARK. PEOPLE EXPERIENCE NIGHT HERE.

THE EARTH'S ROTATION CAUSE THE CHANGE IN TEMPERATURE AND HUMIDITY. IT IS ALSO RESPONSIBLE FOR THE OCCURRENCE OF TIDES IN OCEANS AND SEAS.

REVOLUTION

THE EARTH MOVES AROUND THE SUN IN AN ORBIT WHILE SPINNING ON ITS AXIS. THIS MOVEMENT IS CALLED REVOLUTION.

IT TAKES EARTH 365 DAYS TO COMPLETE ONE ORBIT OF THE SUN. THESE 365 DAYS MAKE A YEAR ON EARTH.

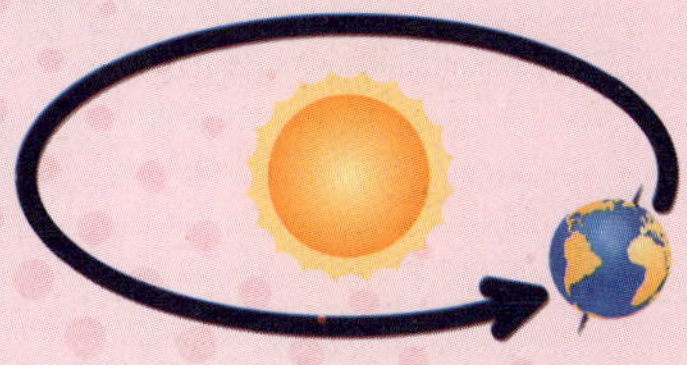

THE REASON FOR SEASONS

THE EARTH'S AXIS AND ITS REVOLUTION AROUND THE SUN CAUSE SEASONS. WE HAVE FOUR MAIN SEASONS

SPRING SUMMER WINTER AUTUMN

DUE TO THE EARTH'S TILTED AXIS, THE SUN'S RAYS HIT DIFFERENT PARTS OF THE EARTH UNEVENLY DURING DIFFERENT TIMES OF THE YEAR.

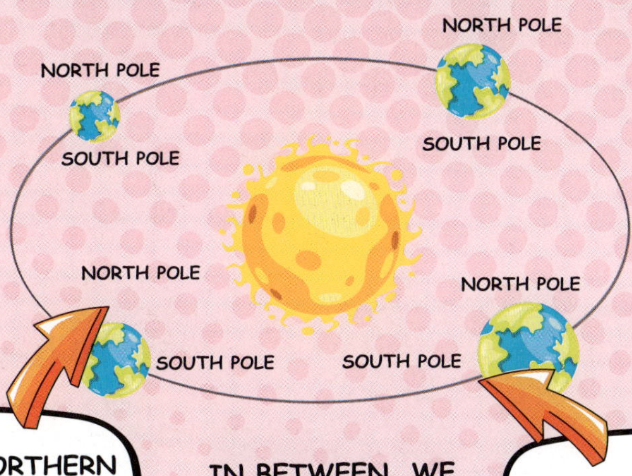

WHEN THE NORTHERN HEMISPHERE IS TILTED TOWARDS THE SUN, IT EXPERIENCES SUMMER.

IN BETWEEN, WE EXPERIENCE THE SEASONS, SPRING AND FALL TOO.

WHILE THE SOUTHERN HEMISPHERE WHICH IS LEANING AWAY, EXPERIENCES WINTER.

ATMOSPHERE

AIR IS ALL AROUND US. IT CANNOT BE SEEN OR TOUCHED BUT ONLY FELT WHEN IT BLOWS.

OUR PLANET IS SURROUNDED BY LAYERS OF AIR CALLED THE ATMOSPHERE.

OUR ATMOSPHERE IS MADE UP OF A NUMBER OF GASES. THESE INCLUDE,

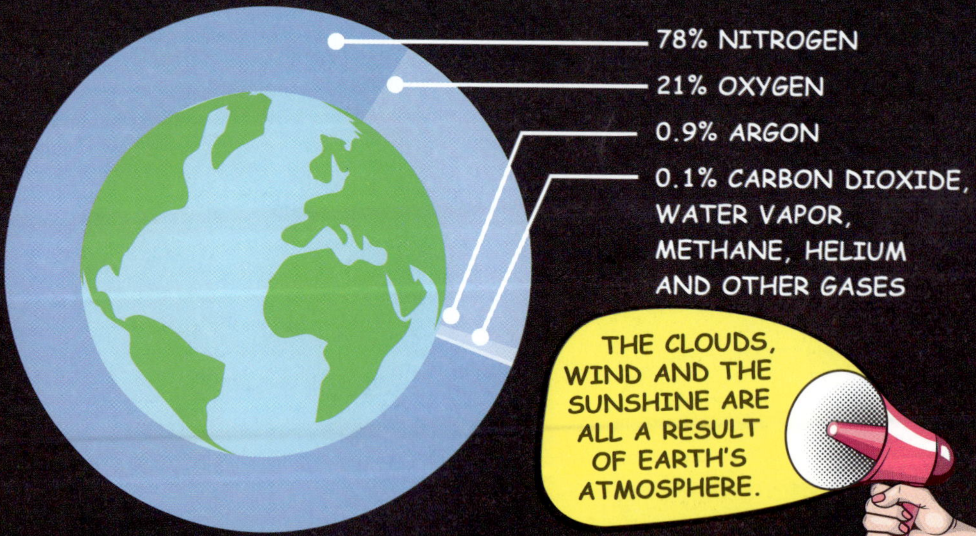

THE CLOUDS, WIND AND THE SUNSHINE ARE ALL A RESULT OF EARTH'S ATMOSPHERE.

NEED OF ATMOSPHERE

SUPPORTS LIFE

ATMOSPHERE CONTAINS THE AIR WE BREATHE, WHICH IS ESSENTIAL FOR LIFE TO EXIST ON EARTH.

A PROTECTIVE SHIELD

THE ATMOSPHERE ACTS AS A SHIELD FOR EARTH. IT BLOCKS MOST OF THE ULTRAVIOLET RADIATIONS OF THE SUN FROM REACHING US.

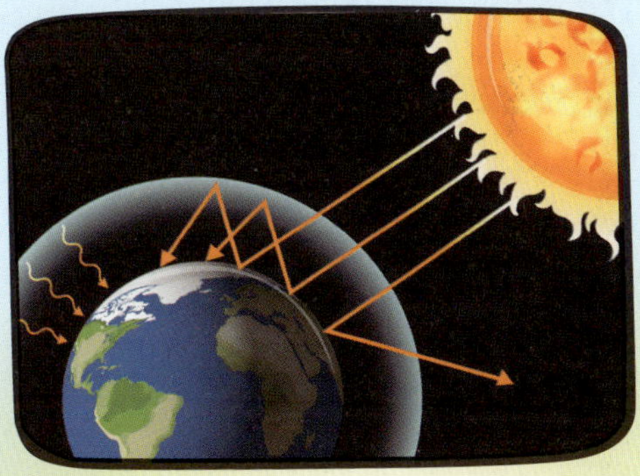

COMFORTABLE TEMPERATURE

IT TRAPS SOLAR HEAT AND LETS IN THE SUNLIGHT WHICH KEEPS EARTH AT A COMFORTABLE TEMPERATURE FOR LIVING BEINGS TO LIVE.

ESSENTIAL FOR WATER CYCLE
ATMOSPHERE HELPS THE MOVEMENT OF WATER ON EARTH.
WATER EVAPORATES OUT OF OCEANS AND OTHER WATER BODIES, CONDENSES AND FORMS CLOUDS, AND FALLS AS RAIN ON THE EARTH.
Condensation
Transpiration
Precipitation
Evaporation
Percolation
CREATES PRESSURE
ATMOSPHERE CREATES PRESSURE WHICH HELPS LIQUID WATER TO EXIST ON EARTH.
WE HEAR SOUNDS
SOUND NEEDS A MEDIUM TO TRAVEL. IT'S BECAUSE OF THE PRESENCE OF AIR, WE HEAR SOUNDS ON EARTH.

LAYERS OF THE ATMOSPHERE

THE ATMOSPHERE IS MADE UP OF SEVERAL LAYERS, OUT OF WHICH FIVE ARE DISTINCT.

THE TROPOSPHERE IS THE DENSEST OF ALL LAYERS. LIFE FORMS AND WEATHER EXIST IN TROPOSPHERE. AIRCRAFTS TOO FLY IN THIS LAYER.

THE OZONE LAYER

THE OZONE LAYER IS A THIN LAYER OF OZONE GAS IN THE ATMOSPHERE. IT IS A PART OF THE SECOND LAYER OF THE ATMOSPHERE, THE STRATOSPHERE.

WHAT IS OZONE MADE OF?

OZONE MOLECULES ARE MADE OF THREE OXYGEN ATOMS. THEY ARE DENOTED BY THE SYMBOL O_3.

A SHIELD

OZONE ABSORBS MOST OF THE ULTRAVIOLET AND OTHER FORMS OF RADIATION THAT COULD BE HARMFUL FOR LIVING BEINGS ON EARTH.

WHAT IF THERE WAS NO OZONE?

WITHOUT THE OZONE LAYER, ULTRAVIOLET RAYS WOULD CAUSE SUNBURNS, DAMAGE THE EYES AND EVEN CAUSE SKIN CANCER.

THE WORD OZONE HAS BEEN DERIVED FROM THE GREEK WORD 'OZEIN' WHICH MEANS 'SMELL'.

WEATHER AND CLIMATE

WEATHER IS THE CONDITION OF AIR AND SKY, INCLUDING WIND, TEMPERATURE, PRESSURE, HUMIDITY, ETC. WEATHER CAN BE SUNNY WITH CLEAR SKIES, COLD OR RAINY.

WHAT CAUSES WEATHER?

THE EFFECT OF SUN AND MOVEMENT OF AIR CAUSES WEATHER ON EARTH.

FIVE ELEMENTS OF WEATHER

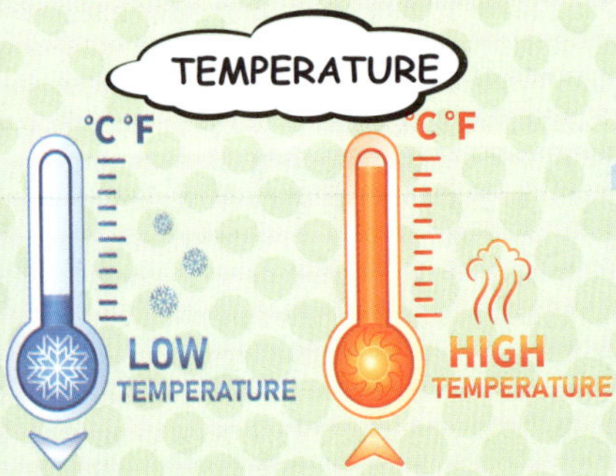

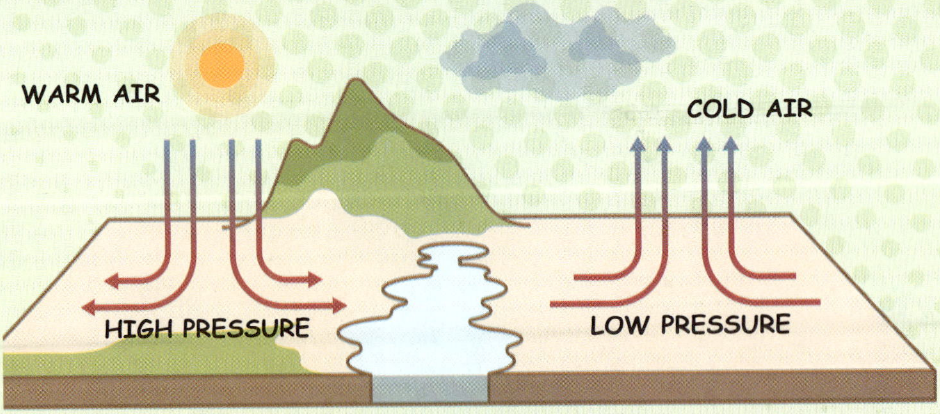

WHAT IS CLIMATE?

CLIMATE IS A PATTERN OF WEATHER AT A PLACE OVER A LONG PERIOD OF TIME. THE CLIMATE OF A PLACE DETERMINES WHAT KIND OF PLANTS AND ANIMALS CAN LIVE THERE.

IT ALSO TELLS US THE BEST TIME TO VISIT THAT PLACE.

WEATHER FORECASTING

WEATHER FORECASTING MEANS TO KNOW HOW THE WEATHER OF A PLACE WOULD BE EACH DAY, FOR A FEW DAYS OR WEEKS.

PEOPLE WHO STUDY WEATHER AND MAKE FORECASTS ARE CALLED METEOROLOGISTS.

THEY PREDICT WEATHER WITH THE HELP OF SATELLITES ORBITING THE EARTH.

SATELLITES ORBITING THE EARTH TAKE PICTURES OF THE EARTH AND HELP SCIENTISTS STUDY THE WEATHER CONDITIONS.

GLOBES AND MAPS

GLOBES AND MAPS ARE TOOLS USED FOR STUDYING THE EARTH AND PLACES ON IT.

THE FIRST KNOWN GLOBE WAS CREATED BY CRATES OF MALLUS IN 2ND CENTURY BC.

A GLOBE HELPS US TO UNDERSTAND THE EARTH'S TILT AND RELATES IT TO THE OCCURRENCE OF DAY, NIGHT AND SEASONS. IT SHOWS SURFACE FEATURES, CONTINENTS, OCEANS, SEAS AND COUNTRIES.

A MAP IS A DRAWING OF SELECTED CHARACTERISTICS OF A PLACE ON A FLAT SURFACE.

MAPS ARE EASIER TO UNDERSTAND AS THEY PRESENT INFORMATION IN A SIMPLE WAY. THEY ARE USED FOR STUDYING:

DISTANCE BETWEEN PLACES

SIZE AND SHAPE OF COUNTRIES

PEOPLE WHO CREATE MAPS ARE CALLED CARTOGRAPHERS.

PHYSICAL FEATURES OF A PLACE SUCH AS RIVERS, LANDFORMS, FORESTS, ETC.
INDONESIA
TIMOR-LESTE
Arafura Sea
Timor Sea
Darwin
INDIAN OCEAN
Gulf of Carpentaria
PAPUA NEW GUINEA
New Guinea
Port Moresby
Coral Sea
NORTHERN TERRITORY
AUSTRALIA
WESTERN AUSTRALIA
QUEENSLAND
SOUTH AUSTRALIA
NEW SOUTH WALES
VICTORIA
Brisbane
Sydney
Canberra
Melbourne
Adelaide
Perth
Alice Springs
Great Australian Bight
Bass Strait
Tasman Sea
Tasmania
INDIAN OCEAN

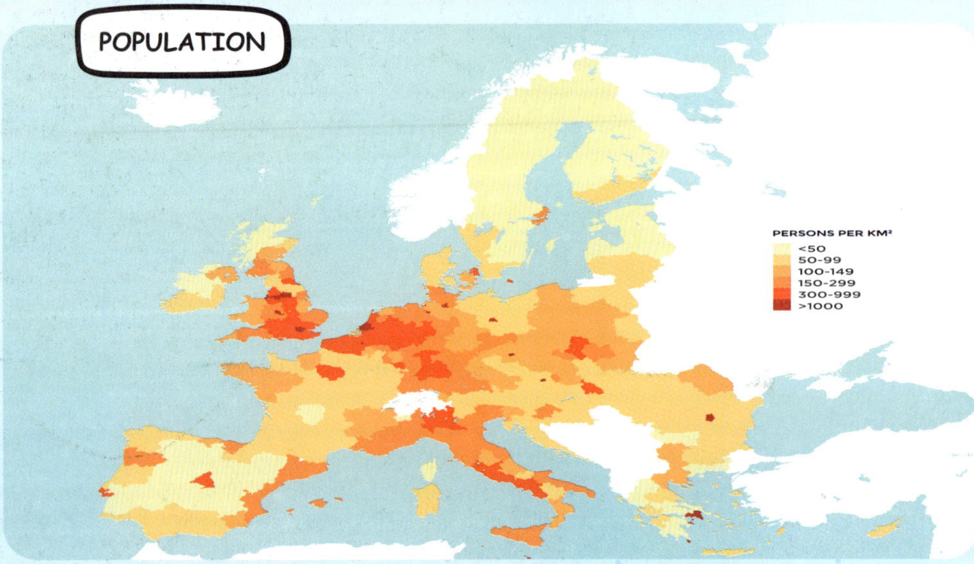
POPULATION
PERSONS PER KM²
<50
50-99
100-149
150-299
300-999
>1000

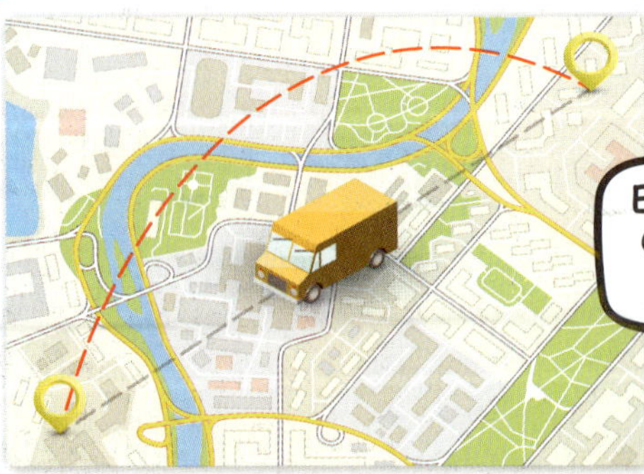
EXACT LOCATION OF HOUSES AND STREETS